WOW!

The Good News in Four Words

written by **Dandi Daley Mackall**

illustrated by **Annabel Tempest**

TYNDALE KIDS

Tyndale House Publishers, Inc.
Carol Stream, IL

For Ellie, Cassie, and Maddie . . . and all God's children

Visit Tyndale's website for kids at www.tyndale.com/kids.

Visit Dandi Daley Mackall online at www.dandibooks.com.

TYNDALE is a registered trademark of Tyndale House Publishers, Inc. The Tyndale Kids logo is a trademark of Tyndale House Publishers, Inc.

Wow!: The Good News in Four Words

Copyright © 2017 by Dandi A. Mackall. All rights reserved.

The concept for this book is based on a sermon by Matt Woodley.

Illustrations by Annabel Tempest. Copyright © Tyndale House Publishers, Inc. All rights reserved.

Designed by Jacqueline L. Nuñez

Edited by Stephanie Rische

Scripture quotations are taken from the *Holy Bible*, New Living Translation, copyright © 1996, 2004, 2015 by Tyndale House Foundation. Used by permission of Tyndale House Publishers, Inc., Carol Stream, Illinois 60188. All rights reserved.

For manufacturing information regarding this product, please call 1-800-323-9400.

For more information about special discounts for bulk purchases, please contact Tyndale House Publishers at csresponse@tyndale.com, or call 1-800-323-9400.

ISBN 978-1-4964-1814-2

Printed in China

23	22	21	20	19	18	17
7	6	5	4	3	2	1

Note to Parents

The gospel is often called "the Good News," and that's because it's the best news ever! God loves us so much that he sent his only Son to pay for our sin by dying for us. Then Jesus rose from the dead, proving that if we believe and accept what Christ has done for us, we can be made right with God and have eternal life. Wow!

The Good News is profound yet simple. Jesus prayed this prayer: "O Father, Lord of heaven and earth, thank you for hiding these things from those who think themselves wise and clever, and for revealing them to the childlike" (Matthew 11:25). This book conveys God's amazing grace and plan of salvation in simple terms children (and grown-ups) will understand and remember.

As you read through each part of this story, encourage your child to shout out each focus word:

Wow! Uh-oh. Yes! Ahh. Wow!

Wow: God, the Creator, loves us (see John 3:16; John 1:1-5).

Uh-oh: We have all sinned, and the result is a broken world and separation from God (see Romans 3:23).

Yes: Jesus died for us and rose from the dead. Through him, we are offered forgiveness and a new beginning . . . if we say yes (see Ephesians 2:8-9; Romans 5:9).

Ahh: Saying yes to Jesus gives us eternal life and peace (see Acts 3:19-20).

Wow: As we grow in faith, we'll want to tell others the Good News (see Matthew 28:18-19).

Back in the beginning, the world was still dark.

No light and no lightning—not even a spark!

No schools and no houses, no playground or park.

3

Then, **WOW!** All God did was say, "Let there be light!"

He called the light "day," and the dark he called "night."

The world God created was perfect and right.

4

Look up in the sky, because here comes the sun!

At night count the stars, if you can, one by one.

Then gaze at the moon and say, "**WOW,** God! Well done."

Just look at the wonders that God had in store,

Like birds, fish, and tigers, and horses and more!

WOW! Creatures with two legs, and creatures with four!

And then God made people—a woman, a man.

For Adam and Eve were both part of God's plan.

They lived in God's Garden. That's where life began.

WOW!

6

Now Adam and Eve had the world at their feet!

The Garden of Eden held every treat

And only one tree from which no one could eat.

Along came the snake, who was bad as could be.

"Did God say, 'Don't eat'? You should listen to *me*.

That fruit is the best!" And Eve chose to agree.

9

So Eve took a bite. **Uh-oh.** Adam did too.

And God saw it all. "Children, what did you do?"

Since then, we all sin. That means me. That means you.

We have to say, **"Uh-oh."** We're in a bad place.

We can't earn God's favor or talk face-to-face.

We're helpless and hopeless, in need of God's grace.

Wow! Uh-oh.

Yes

But God had a wonderful, masterful plan:

"I'll pay for their sin, because only I can.

I'll save the whole world . . . by becoming a man."

God loved us so much that he sent us his Son.

So Jesus was born, and the plan was begun.

His life was just perfect. No sin. No, not one.

Yet people grew jealous. "Don't trust him! Beware!"

They had him arrested. His trial was unfair.

He died on a cross. He was crucified there.

14

But that's not the end! Jesus rose from the dead!

He came back to life again, just like he said,

And gave us a promise of what lies ahead.

For Christ is the Life and the Truth and the Way

For all who believe and receive him today.

Say, "Yes!" and your new life begins right away.

Wow! Uh-oh. Yes!

Ahh

Our life is in Jesus, our very best Friend!

He'll always be with us, right up to the end.

For we have the Spirit he promised to send.

With Jesus beside us, there's nothing to fear.

No matter what happens, our Savior is near.

Then when we're in heaven, he'll wipe every tear.

We'll join all the angels in heaven to sing,

"All praise to the Father and Jesus the King!

The Ruler of heaven, who made everything!"

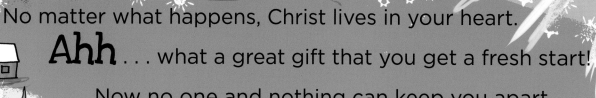

No matter what happens, Christ lives in your heart.

Ahh . . . what a great gift that you get a fresh start!

Now no one and nothing can keep you apart.

Wow! Uh-oh. Yes! **Ahh.**

20

WOW

The fruit of the Spirit that's in you will grow.

Now love, joy, and patience are starting to show.

You walk with the Savior wherever you go.

21

Be thankful for Jesus. Let love overflow.

Tell others God loves them. The world needs to know!

And sharing this news helps your own faith to grow.

WOW!
Uh-oh.
Yes!
Ahh.
WOW!

24

For Further Study

Parents, if you want to dig deeper into the gospel with your child (or on your own), here are some Scripture passages that address the ideas in each part. Of course, you can find many more verses throughout the Bible that talk about God's plan for us, but these may give you a place to start.

Genesis 1–2

Psalm 19:1-6

Psalm 24:1-2

Psalm 33:6-9

John 1:1-5

Uh-Oh

Psalm 25:11

Psalm 41:4

Psalm 51:1-14

Romans 3:12

Romans 3:23-26

Romans 5:19-21

Yes

John 3:16

Romans 5:6-9

Romans 6:8

Ephesians 2:8-9

1 Thessalonians 5:9

1 John 5:11-12

Ahh

Psalm 16:5-11

John 14:27

1 Peter 5:7

1 John 5:13-15

Revelation 7:17

Revelation 21:4

Matthew 28:18-20

Galatians 5:22-23

Colossians 2:7

Colossians 3:16-17

1 John 4:7